Shoot the Stars

By

Paul Billett

PublishAmerica
Baltimore

First printing

ISBN: 1-4241-2815-3
PUBLISHED BY PUBLISHAMERICA, LLLP
www.publishamerica.com
Baltimore

Printed in the United States of America

Ace of Spades

As the cards are dealt
Your eyes start to melt
To join the human race
Card flys out an ace
From a journey to outer space
Love a seven of hearts or two
A heart to whom concerns
A heart to yearn
Message in love to learn
Heart to chase an ace
A face to face in honest taste
In money to fund a diamond
In love to condescend.

Angels

The view from an angel's eyes
To see a heavenly glance
Is a beautiful chance to enhance
Angels in full flight, who gently touch my face
And lift me to the sky
Seven rainbows surround the view
Seven angels to paint the colours
So serene, so pure in love's cure.

Ascendent

Rising in the east the sun
Outward appearance and impression upon
Purely physical an outlook and behaviour all related
The traits not hated
The subject with control is controlled
Directions are modified levels rolled
To influence the ascendent time just went,
With all the power heaven sent.

Blessing

The blessing of a summer's day
Tranquil and serene
The blood does flow as the sun shines
The way the day forever in thought to stay
The presence of the moment to seize
Is in heart glad to please
The blessing of a summer's day
Tranquil and serene is good to write good to ease
Memories are remembered not to cease
The future is to unfold
And we would be happy for a blessing of a summer's day to be
told.

Borrowing Peace

Do we pay for peace?
Do we steal for peace?
Do we work for a piece at last?
Does this tale ring for borrowing
Inanimate oneself a cartoon
World destruction soon
Self evident self worth
A bee stings
Borrowing peace, borrowing time
The peace is mine
God above will call time
A puzzle a rhyme.

Circle Forever

A ring of truth circles ahead,
A man writes all is read,
A circle so strong and bold,
Unbroken promises are meant to be,
I believe what I see,
And I see a ring of truth
Spins around with light
Dark shadow, snow white
Halo hey high all right
Stars in eyes at night
Twinkle to sing
Not big a little king
King pin wears the white ring
War swords turn to words
Next to worlds of wisdom
Forword spelt wrong
Derails an impact of
thought,
Forward march fights in magnifying memory
Circle forever just balance not clever
No difference just intense,
To fence with wit,
We watch and sit.

Clouds of Confusion

The clouds of confusion confuse
Sunlight's rays to break through
Rain pours the pain to wash away
Clouds are gone suns to see to stay
Warmth caresses us with warmth
Clear skies of blue to hew
Rainbows enhance with colour to you
A fusion not to confuse to you
Now is now, you choose.

Cold

I lay here cold,
My clothes all sold
I hold on to what
So cold wish for a hot spot
I cry where's my lover I cry a river
Cold so cold, warmth a giver
Alas I see her I want to grasp
Now she holds me tight
My heart dances so alight
Kisses my cold lips shivers in love
I stand and hold in love above
My lover I love, cold winds that shook
I stand here warm,
The cold she took.

Conclusion

As the day enfolds
Into a crystal clear thought
The love that inspires us so sought
Happiness is a border of dimensions
As the light turns the corners
The darkness that runs
Time stops for a second of an hour
Past images seduce the minute
The conclusion of comparisons
In the end time just fits.

Crystal Clear World

The waters of a thought are abstract to the eye
To think clear thoughts of a crystal that fly
A ball resolves a cloud of emotion
Silver lines the pocket of the rich
What ever concludes for ever a switch
Turns crystal surrounding the mist
To cover the lids of beauty prevail
Prevails a veil to sail the sea
For we are free to be, no fight
A right to express with sight
For peace is crystal clear no sword
O a crystal clear world.

Dawn

To sense the day,
Waking from the womb of night
To feel your way
Breathing in the day's new light
Your mind begins to stir
Eyes mirror and explore
This entrance to the world about
Its colours beyond the door
Is the day beginning?
Or is this the end of the night?
Does it really matter?
It's within our realm of sight
Our fears rekindled
Our hopes to the fore
This resolves with us once more.

Drawing White Lines

Drawing white balls,
In a black atmosphere of fools
White balls, orbs
Electricity absorbs
Communication lost in space
Misread words deface pace
A spire a fire logs frozen in pain
Frozen pain rains reigns the reins
Resigns in words of wisdom that mean what
To clear the decks
Ships yes wrecked cards burnt
Tables of numbers only count in opportunity
To count the white lines a ball of string
How long do we go on
A line is a line only breaks to black
Draw a white line strong and fine
To cross a border of yours or mine
In essence is just mumble jumble
Straight words straight lines
Drawing white lines.

Energy of Space

The energy of space
That is surrounded by the energy
Of a border of visionary illusion
That shines into the eyes of rage of age
As the space is broken down
The squares of a dimension of an universe
With the rays of a light
From a day to a night
Planets spin from left to right
Up, down, below, and with height
Length, width all in sight
Gases amass with critical acclaim
Energy of space forms a race
Colours combine, refined so fine a face
Hands are handed down
From space to energy
From nothing to a black mist
Created to an iron fist.

Eyes All Around

Eyes are surrounding the walls,
Bouncing of rays of sight
Cross rays of light
Different lines of thought of a wall
Bricks that block the way we thrive forward toward
Eyes look down now on earth's ground there's no sound
Time is lost in three dimensions only to look up
Emotions know what we've got, not a lot to show
To build a bridge of rays of eyes all around on ground
We walk the light of insight
To believe in something we can't touch
We feel our way upwards to look down
A vision of walls shaped to a square in air
All eyes round all around.

Fire of Flames

The flames that burn fires of hot emotion
Candles flicker a hope of wind of change
Blue flames turn to yellow red in rage
Black coals lost souls
Green lights the holes touches close
Flying embers of spits of energy
Blinds the eyes never to see
Feel the heat to inflame
Cold is forgotten old and lame
Fire of flames the name.

Imagination

To be alive to see the sky so blue
Is precious far between so few
Beauty of wonders the colours so bright
Imagination of a mind of insight
Views of a paradise lost in time
A riddle has formed for answers to show
To be fast or slow
Imagination draws a picture so serene
On times that have been.

Levels of Society

An outcast into solitude and confinement
Medication stops the pain flowing into cement
Drains the soul of love so sought
Good words enhance the action with creative thoughts
Builds the blocks of a creative world to last
To create a paradise that is lost in the past
To unwind red tape the laws are analysed and reformed to see
To form a logical positive idea wide and so free.

Lie Down

As I lie down to rest in sleep,
And wonder of good memories lost in time
My bottle my master of disaster
So much water, that I shed in tears
As I squander in sorrow in years
Good times gone, bad times lead
Self pity self worth from death to birth
Awakens the eyes in sights
My bottle the master, gives life
But when in reality I wake in strife
No cares no worries in my sad life.

Life Mine

This is my life to life,
As I battle the thoughts of a battle of strife
The need for speed so slow the war of weeds
Digging a hole of holes plants magic seeds
Needs speeds weeds magic seeds feeds the needs
With the art paints a start with beating heart
The heart to chase the beats defeats the heat
This is my life to live to life
The streets speak no names
To speak just shames the games
A player a frame shoots the ball's lightening speed
The weed to feed the need to spark
Memories of hate sinks the ark
A dog bites the bone, laughter barks
A tale to tale of all infernos to hell to tell
Oh well so well jets of steam dampen hell
Don't lose to choose, just spread the news.

Love Breaks

The flash of thunder bolts my heart
Horses running love parts
Would you bet to lose
We choose our track of choice
To listen to our inner voice
Snap bang a broken part departs
Crazy days in my head can I win
World spins ever on as my head spins
Against the odds a miracle I call
My horse falls
I cry a waterfall of pain
Time eases the pain in warm rain
My pain takes as the love breaks
My family always there
To wrap around a circle of love
And wipe my tears away
But memories of love forever I say.

Love, Passion, Faith and Belief

To laugh in the face of adversity
To travel a cloud of thought
To search for understanding is taught
Knowledge that teaches away fear
For to know is to hear
To listen to see takes away the tear
As great philosophers inspire into great men
The block that slows down time
To push hard and yet not move
For passion and love not to prove
To move mountains to one side
The answer not to hide
To show true feelings with no loss
As the great teacher man on cross
The passion still grows, time the healer
Born is a new leaf
With love, passion, faith, belief.

Moment in Time

Running from time
A man pays for peace
In honesty or a golden feast
A self-war of hate
Self imaged fate
Seizes the moment in glory
To tell his life story
A tale to tell
Into paradise from hell
The sun burns a ray
Lights a fire to desire
Bottom to top to higher
Broken face turns the card to face
An ace to grace.

Myself

As I walk the earth through trouble and strife
I look in the mirror at life, and myself
There are footsteps where a man walked before
Did he end at the start or start at the end?
I see a rainbow not black or white, what a sight
I hear a voice of fear I must go now
I look ahead I see a lady maybe
As I walk on my eyes open to see
For in the distance grows a powerful strong tree
Negativity I shun
As I think in four dimensions
Darkness borders the light
Freedom rebels, on hill on high
As I walk the earth past trouble and strife
And think what a miracle, the thing called life.

Patterns

Self depressing signs in the soul
General issues aired to repaired
As the judgment is impaired
The lows and highs are recognized
Eyes to eyes, to see not to hide
As inner thoughts are internally free
The patterns emerge and are no fret
And all emotions, the needs are met
A letter grasps in all is sent to stamp out sin
As we build the blocks to comment to win
Our inner and outer spaces are meant
A picture emerges so confident
All bad memories, so easy just went.

Poetry in Motion

For others to perceive to see
In reflection of how you would hope to see them yourself
An image of a worldly wave
Illusion to cover all nations
For battles to cease at all stations
To perceive to believe in positive reaction
By first steps in healthy action
To see all to stand tall
And all backward motion to fall
Is indeed poetry in motion?
For perfume in potion
For all weak to rise
To grow strong the prize a rose
And all boundaries join to those?
The mirror reflects a vision of us
To look poor? Or full of wealth?
A treasure of life to live
To love to give
A notion an idea
To look, to touch, to hear
A touch of class, wood on glass
For fortune to appear alas
Sword to a pen
Poetry in motion only then.

Ray of Light

The day was caressed by a ray of light
That opened the eyes to a cosmic sight
The stars on planets far away
For the journey of life to stay
The first beginning a spark of light
That lights the dark night
The end, the start, to start to end
The cosmic light for it does bend
For the warmth is caressed
For the heavens to send
Time does beat for all to meet
A jigsaw is a piece, to piece the part
In a world of light to ignite the pure heart.

Realms of Reality

To realms of reality
To the realms of a dream
Different worlds, different streams
The water of life, a fountain of hope
To break the doors of a universe
Is music to the ears of life's verse?
The dark with shadows
The day sun bright glows
To the realms of reality a dream
As the water pours in life's stream.

Rivers

The rivers that flow
As night broadens into a cascade of living glow
Surrounds the eye up, down on high to show
The picture with rainbow colours
So taint, falls down a golden fountain
Rivers to flow
On it passes on it goes
The sun glimmers as the river creates a mirror of an age
No rage to cease for the river settles into a calm full of peace.

I See God

I was walking along the woods two angels by my side,
The sun shining through the trees,
Small creatures, curious hide,
So beautiful to please,
In a flash a man appeared,

I asked "who are you in front of me?"
The look in his eyes so warm
"I am God, can't you see"
A buzz, ten thousand bees, a swarm
Took the light in front
A man appeared
The devil his hunt
The devil behind, God ahead, steered
God spoke "don't turn your back, my son
"For what is ahead is love
"And what is behind is hate
"Walk with me and I will take you above
"Yes I will 24th the date."

I was walking along the wood two angels by my side
24th the date my birthday reborn
I don't look back in anger, look forward to love to God
The devil I scorn
In the sky the clouds spelt always remember me
It was so clear to see
I love God, now I'm free
He showed me the way
Now the memory for God will forever stay.

Seven Gold Coins

Coins I found on the way
As I walked on a summer's day
The man had gone, loved in heaven
These coins gold all seven shining
With help from the sun
Was this luck? Was this fate?
The time? The month? The date?
Seven gold coins what did it mean?
What did it seem to mean?
Was this real? Was it a dream? Of dreams?
This treasure to pleasure,
But which way to go?
Do I keep to reap? Or sell to weep?
These seven gold coins had made me think and wonder,
What to do, be a man or shrew?
These thoughts are far and far between,
I will keep my thoughts clear,
For this is not a dream to me,
This is real reality and I'm going to be me,
I kept these seven gold coins,
Now I'm happy as a man can be.

Shoot the Stars

The fire inside me, volcano boom,
You hit me with your tongue,
So sharp, if you were a fish, a sword fish,
You would be?????
Don't hit me for I will fire back,
Now I've got the knack,
On your bike, chuck the tic tacs,
Pitter-patter too much natter,
See me I'm doing fine, just passing the time,
Time to time, when I fire back at you
I will send you to Venus
I've got the power, to shoot you with the stars
Don't think it's fun or I will shoot from the sun
The sun the stars, not that on mars
Get back to the bar, you're going too far
Chill a bit or I will chuck you in the pit
You're not fit to hit me with your soul
Underground you go, live with the moles
Darkness, no life, you're not fit to be my wife
I don't give a hoot
For the stars they are going to shoot your heart
I've got the art, this is my play
So away you go, take your tongue in tow
Below, below, you go
I win, you sin
Now I win to sin.

Shooting Sparkles

The sun beams down rays of sparkles
The sea is flowing a wave of love
Rain lights down a shooting might
Sparkles shout towards the beach
A sight to remember so perfect to reach
Sparkles into stars, bouncing in the day
As I rest down my hat I lay
Relaxed not taxed awake, asleep
Benefits pour down to reap
Sparkles shooting stars
Past conjunction planet mars.

Simple Truth

The simple truth is only a word,
That makes the world spin around
And simply keeps feet on the ground
To wonder in a silent thought
As the years grow as we are taught
Wars are at fault to be frozen in time
The simple truth a nursery rhyme
Rhythm, space the beat of a heart
All these visions play a part
The simple truth there it is
And there we are
As one was started, that one a star.

Sky

The clouds of white fluffiness
That wraps around and covers the earth in total solitude
To elude the dark mood, to cover the light
The clouds that shine and put others to shame
With a shine of hope to cope to break the impossible truth
The sky with glimpses of light that infatuates the sight
With all its might
Flying clouds of thought, clouds of fluffiness.

Smiles

All the frowns and downs of being alone
When the skin is shredded to the bone
All the tears that drown a sea of ghosts
Then love appears a boat of golden hosts
To ride the wave of hearts
Sails a hundred miles
With a sun of smiles
A moment to cure, so pure
I love her with a silver anchor
Feet touch the ground, musical sound
A thousand red roses cover the land for miles
As I walk by with a sun's smile.

Snow

Snow so white
Falls in falls of beauty
A frozen waterfall that breaks at night
White light in balls of flight
Impression of cold stars against the black sky
Touches the land into a blanket
Earth to snow touched down
As the world was wearing a white dressing gown.

Sparkling Crystals

The water of life
Sparkles in crystals
And shines a sparkling jewel
With eyes wide open to see
A sea of glass clear as crystal
A fountain of rain I saw
Springs of a vision of love so tall
Seven stars give light to separate with might
Water so clear
Cleanses the soul of fear
Sparkles in crystals
Shines a sparkling jewel
A diamond turns to a pearl
Gives life to death a price so priceless.

Super Nova

A super nova star so bright
Twinkles in the midnight sky
Conversations on earth is write
To burn the candle
Birds in flight
The air is fresh and cleans the thought
The constellations host a variety of lights
As the night turns to day
All the love is to reap
As we talk the stars to sleep.

The Day

The sea air does swirl in a relaxed twirl
The air so fresh that the salt does fly by
Activities are above to enhance the time
The free are free to have and is fine
As the day passes and time is timed
The picture changes as in art
The colours are shaded with the sun in full glow
What beauty is not to behold
No lies it is just told
What a day what a way
Love this day seize it
And in your mind it will stay.

The Flight of Light

The flight of light
In morning sight
The horizon burns a flaming sun
Surrenders the contrast of the dark
Ignition pushes, rushes a spark
A reflection, a comparison of time
The whole world does shine
Scenery the eye with sight of sun
A beautiful dimension on horizon.

The Wall

The woman with mixed intentions
Stuck in a world of spinning tops
Take the cork out
Pop, she can't take the pace
She has four hands on the clockface
Doesn't know what the time is, or the day
Or what she has to say
Destruction built the bridge over the wall
The bridge it fell, now she is stale
You can hear the whale
What can I do to beat these blocks?
What's the time on the clock?
My mind's set like rock
I'm all alone, heart set in stone
The robot, the drone needs some help to beat these blues
There's some news I knew, phew
I can see the red rose and the thorn I am reborn, into a world of
innocence
Have a toast I'm no longer a ghost
What a fright turned on the light
Now I spin, spin to win
I don't want tin, I'm after gold, I feel bold, not young not old
I did as I was told, from the rose to the grave
Next time I am here I will think from rags to riches, from mice to
stags, from a beagle
To a soaring eagle
For I can see and see I will
The pot will fill, the wind still, rain will not pain, the sun will
shine, for I am full of
Life's rich vain
The wall will fall, for I will love and love I will
The clock will tick to punch that brick, for I am one and one is all.

Total Eclipse

The moment of total eclipse
As I kiss her sweet lips
The sweetness that fills the air
The time we both share
This is advanced in a magical dance
The passion is to entrance
Total tranquillity the peace still
Two hearts are entwined
The look in both eyes transfixed
In a lustful and provocative stare
As a lion restless in his lair
Sweet antidotes dissipates hate
For this is a time of a romantic hour
For the hearts to beat in time with time
As a chime to alarm the pain,
As the sun shines to dissapear,
The rain.

Twisting Time

Unscrew the bottle
For a twist in time
I drank fate all mine
From love to hate in it came
Out came the rain with pain
Anxious feelings sped to lose
That did I choose but to lose
Keep it in I can't win
Twisting the top
Dived in the water a flop
Honest and true too
Heart hurts so much
Only drank my pain away
Next day I think it stays all day what a way
Only had a drink to drown
Lost my love my world upside down
Fault all mine, twisting time.

War Sounds

The beats of a thousand drums echoes in the distance
Ten thousand trumpets blow a tune to trance
Thunder snaps in time
Lightning awakes the soldiers all in line
Lancers edge the hill static dancers
Guns are cold the young and old
The rain is pouring onto the mud
With a whip of a moment will change red covered with blood
Sounds of horror sounds of glory
All the peace in life's story
When all is won and the battle to cease
Silence is born and won is the peace.

War

The soldier that went to war
The memories of pain he saw
Came back broken in two
He was valiant, for me for you
He fights back tears now
Tears of remorse, of woe
He wipes off the flashbacks
For the heart he does not lack
The love he builds day to day
He knows depression might stay
He asks the lord to forgive
The lord says you live
Find the heart from now on
For you fight for peace
So now let anger release
All the pain to cease
For you have asked
Now your heart is grasped
What you need is to sow the seed
Bless you, my son, for you have won
From this day in your eyes
Your soul will blaze like the sun.

Wars Among the Stars

A war of stars of armies of lights
Cross paths of darkness to defeat
Suns of desire of fire of heat
A battle of science no brains rattle
Emerges our time to think it through
Battles commence the speed of light I rate
Time against the war is too late for fate
Time to time joins the rhythm
All stars against the stars
Watched on TV in all the bars
Even on mars, those bars
Joined no holds, chocolate just folds
Space related my father watched too
All planets may disappear soon
But at least for we have the moon.

Water on Fire

Light the water in rays of fire
Steam echoes in rings of a liar
Echoes truth in ripples
Oxygen injects in life
To air waves no strife
The water colours a rainbow trout
Hook line and sinker
Rings of fire are all about
Bubbles of troubles pop out the old
To break the moment just been sold
Steams of streams, awaken all's dreams.

White Horses

The sea awakes in waves of movements
Swirling motions, the wind is sent
The boats are sailing different courses
The crest of a wave broken white horses
White horses ride, the waves chanting
Galloping in glorious crescendos
The waves in line, all in a row
Battering the rocks to submission
The white horses disappear
The sea is serene and clear
The sun goes down the stars awake
Mirrored images on seas and lakes
To sea to sea in all its beauty
From all God's creatures, the free and free.

White Snow

A winter's day
As the clouds grow dark
As the snow falls down in white flakes
As it covers the land the white it makes
Footsteps are where creatures have walked
And others follow on as stalked
The white snow falls over all as the land glistens from the sun
All the children outside play with glorious fun
A naturally made toy from a winter's day
The sun melts to thaw as the night arrives
And the dark is silent in magical arrival
An owl calls out as to sound the silence
All this on a winter's day on show
With the fall of beautiful white snow.

Who Cares

The crisp awaken of a day's whisk,
Wind breaks covers the acre to care with air,
An air of grace, gives to take,
Creative, creates to make,
Who cares to share,
In a world of greed indeed,
Who wears the airs
A circus, no fairs
Clowns uplift the frowns
Lords are swinging, swings of balance
Devils, no cares in there dance
Animals play the second fiddle,
In the band of nature
Who graces in airs to care
A tone but not alone with or without
A master in mind takes care the shout
Care takes over the show
Curtain shuts tight the stage
Who cares?

Wings of Flight

As the wings of flight
Are thrown into a deep hole
You must learn to fly in fast time
And soar and thrust, to reach the top
As you enter the sky
And the wind passes you by,
You shout aloud I'm free so free,
The sun shines on wings of gold
You land on a beach
And touch the ground,
In the distance a beautiful sound,
You look around and shout I'm free
So free so free, world look at me.

World

When the world seems at its worst
Think of all the pain others feel
And this thought it would heal
When the world is at its best
Think of the good and join the rest
When the world is calm and serene
Think of me and read what I mean
When the world is gone from scene
I hope we all learnt to rise above
With words of hope,
And words of goodness, said with love.

You Think

You think of me
In words and pictures
A scene of love
That we both caress
Only past memories no less.

Chorus

You think that I lied and cheated
You think I lost my soul in the heat
Is only my heart that longs to beat
With you together in defeat to love

I think of you
In love and out in love
But you erase pictures in past
It didn't last
Why did it go, insecurity blew away
Good times remain in the ashes.
A fire lights away.

Chorus

Do you remember the first kiss,
Remember the first laugh,
We walked with the sun that day,
Thought it was going to stay,
Rain wiped the picture away.
In a flash of hate.

Chorus

I woke alone today
Seemed a different light
My heart yearns to beat in time
You think I lost my soul
I lost it when I wasn't whole with you
Can't you get it through to you?

Chorus

Printed in the United Kingdom
by Lightning Source UK Ltd.
114956UKS00001B/372

9 781424 128150